Poetry for Reading and Writing

Grades 2-5

by Dorothy P. Hall

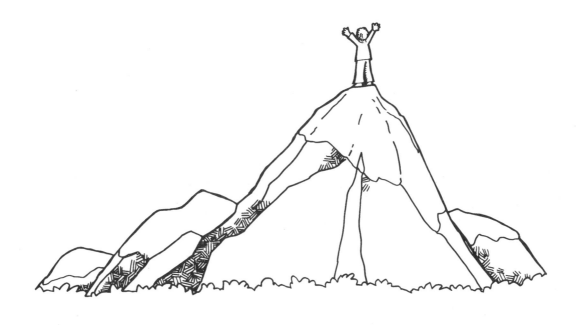

Carson-Dellosa Publishing Company, Inc.
Greensboro, North Carolina

Credits

Editor
Joey Bland

Layout Design
Van Harris

Inside Illustrations
Janet Armbrust

Cover Design
Matthew Van Zomeren

Cover Illustration
Matthew Van Zomeren

ISBN 978-1-59441-792-4

Dedication

This book is dedicated to the wonderful students/student teachers at Wake Forest University who made this book a reality during their senior year (2005).

Katie Ball

Katie Beaver

Katherine Cardwell

Turner Chambliss

Katie Chinlund

Payton Deal

Pattie Gabbert

Rory Gavin

Amanda Gordon

Rebecca Hix

Lorah Hoft

Emily Johnson

Stephen Lyday

Jennifer Place

Martha Ripple

Amelia Rogers

Melanie Schneider

Anna Shaw

Lenora Simpson

Annie Ward

Kandace Wernsing

Annie Young

Table of Contents

Table of Contents

Introduction

Do you like to read and write poetry? Do you think it is fun to teach poetry? The answers to these two questions depend on your prior experiences with poetry. But, if you answered that you don't like to read, write, or teach poetry, how are you going to introduce poetry to students? How are your students going to learn to read and write poetry if it is not included as part of your instruction?

The parents of preschoolers have discovered that young children like the sound of poetry. It seems that the sounds of certain words are very appealing and can catch children's attention or even lull them to sleep at night. Teachers of young children have discovered that poetry helps teach beginning reading, expand language development, and enrich experiences across the curriculum. Researchers have found that poetry memorized in childhood stays in the mind for a lifetime. When children learn poems for a holiday, family occasion, or school project, they can often recite them years later. As children read poems, they often realize the power of poetry. Some poems make them laugh, some poems make them think, and some poems tell stories. Some poems create strong rhythmic beats, and some poems create soothing flows of words.

Teachers need to read poetry to students at every grade level. Young children like the sound of poetry even before they pay attention to what the words say. Teachers need to teach reading strategies with poetry, helping their students understand the poems they read. Teachers in grades two through five should let their students try their hands at writing different types of poetry. Writing poetry can be just as much fun as reading it, and, for some children, writing poetry is even more fun. **This book was written to help teachers do three things: read poetry to children, read poetry with children, and teach children to write poetry.**

Types of Poetry

Poetry can be classified in several ways. One way to classify poems is based on whether the lines rhyme. Poems that rhyme are called rhymed verse. Poems that don't rhyme are called free verse. In the past, traditional poetry rhymed, but many contemporary poems do not. In free verse, imagery, figurative language, and other literary elements are used instead of rhyme. Another way to classify poems is based on poetic forms. Haiku, cinquain, and limerick are types of poems that follow specific forms. A third way to classify poems is based on arrangement of words or lines. Concrete and acrostic are types of poems for which the arrangement matters.

In a concrete poem, the words or lines are arranged on the page to create a design or shape that reinforces the topic of the poem.

If I could fly, I think I'd try to fly so high up in the sky to grab a star and make it mine. Stars are high up in the sky.

In an acrostic poem, the lines are arranged so that the first letters of the lines are combined to spell a word when the letters are read vertically.

Spring

Sunny

Plants

Rain

Insects

Nature

Growing

These two arrangement poems are actually fun for most students to try to write, and they often find success creating these poems even if writing rhymed verse is not among their talents.

Types of Poetry Books

Poetry books published for children fall into four categories. The first type is a picture book in which a line or stanza is illustrated on each page. These are some of the first books parents buy for toddlers and emergent readers. (See page 13 for examples.)

Another type of poetry book for children is a collection of poems written by a single poet. Shel Silverstein's *Where the Sidewalk Ends* (HarperCollins, 1974) and *A Light in the Attic* (HarperCollins, 1981) are examples of poetry books children really enjoy and parents and teachers buy. In years past, *A Child's Garden of Verses* by Robert Louis Stevenson (Simon & Schuster Children's Publishing, 1999) was another popular collection.

The third type is a collection of poems on a certain subject or theme. *Cat Poems* selected by Myra Cohn Livingston (Holiday House, 1987) or *Zoo Doings: Animal Poems* by Jack Prelutsky (Greenwillow Books, 1983) are examples of this type.

The fourth type of poetry book for children is a comprehensive anthology of many poems arranged by category. Two of the best anthologies for children are *The Random House Book of Poetry for Children* selected by Jack Prelutsky (Random House Books for

Young Readers, 2000) and *The 20th Century Children's Poetry Treasury* selected by Jack Prelutsky (Knopf Books for Young Readers, 1999). A good collection of children's poetry has been and always will be a must for elementary teachers.

About This Book

This book touches on reading and writing poetry for children in grades two through five. The concept was formed when students in the education department at Wake Forest University were introduced to teaching poetry in their language arts methods course. The students enjoyed reading and writing some poetry and wanted to share their experiences with other teachers. This book suggests poems that teachers can **read to** their students, poems that teachers can **read with** their students during Guided Reading lessons using a shared or echo reading format, and ideas for writing poetry that elementary teachers can use for models as they try **writing with** their students.

Poetry can be fun. Capture the love your students had for nursery rhymes and have for jump rope chants, raps, and songs. Read all types of poetry by a variety of poets to your students. As you teach students to write through personal narratives, informational pieces, letters, and descriptions, don't stop there. Writing instruction should and can include some fun with poetry. Students will never know if they are poets at heart if you don't give poetry a try in your classroom!

Reading Poetry to Children

When parents and teachers read to young children, the children hear rhymed verse; first in nursery rhymes and then in popular books by Dr. Seuss and many other authors writing especially for toddlers. It is no wonder that many young students think that poetry always rhymes. For students in grades two through five, it is important to take a deeper look at poetry and realize that there is more to poetry than meets the ear. During the teacher read-aloud, students can listen to poetry read by an experienced reader who can help them appreciate the sound of rhymed verse, as well as listen to and learn about poetry written in free verse.

Shel Silverstein

One of the best-loved children's poets is Shel Silverstein. His poetry is fun to read and listen to and brings smiles to both younger and older children. Some of Silverstein's poems are very short and some are longer, but be sure to gather your class close in front of you when reading his poetry because there are illustrations for them to see and enjoy as much as the words. You can share the illustrations while you are reading the poems or right after you finish.

Silverstein's first collection of poems and drawings, *Where the Sidewalk Ends*, was published in 1974 (HarperCollins). Some of the most popular poems to read to students from this collection are:

- "Invitation," page 9
- "Smart," page 35 (A good poem for a math lesson!)
- "For Sale," page 52
- "Sick," page 58
- "Sarah Cynthia Sylvia Stout Would Not Take the Garbage Out," page 70
- "Benjamin Bunnn," page 104
- "Band-Aids," page 140 (Another wonderful poem for a math lesson!)

Silverstein's second collection of poetry and drawings, *A Light in the Attic,* was published in 1981 (HarperCollins). Some favorite poems to read and share with students are:

- "Hammock," page 10
- "Homework Machine," page 56
- "Gumeye Ball," page 68
- "Crowded Tub," page 86
- "Whatif," page 90
- "The Fly Is In," page 100

Classic Poetry

Many teachers want their students to read and appreciate the "classic" poems and poets. Sterling Publishing has recently published a series of books—Poetry for Young People— that contain collections of poems by some well-known poets. Although these poems were originally written for adults, teachers can share them with elementary students. Included in the series are works by Robert Frost, Emily Dickinson, Walt Whitman, Edgar Allan Poe, William Carlos Williams, Carl Sandburg, and many others. Most of the books in the series are collections of rhymed verse and are pleasing to listen to when read by a skilled reader or someone who has previously read them. The poems aren't amusing like Shel Silverstein's but can bring pictures to your students' minds.

- *Poetry for Young People: Carl Sandburg* edited by Frances Schoonmaker Bolin (1995)
- *Poetry for Young People: Edgar Allan Poe* edited by Brod Bagert (1995)
- *Poetry for Young People: Emily Dickinson* edited by Frances Schoonmaker Bolin (1994)
- *Poetry for Young People: Robert Frost* edited by Gary D. Schmidt (1994)
- *Poetry for Young People: Walt Whitman* edited by Jonathan Levin (1997)
- *Poetry for Young People: William Carlos Williams* edited by Christopher MacGowan (2003)

Songs, Raps, and Riddles

Because poetry is no longer confined to rhyming verse, it now includes songs, raps, word pictures, memories, riddles, and observations. So, take advantage of songs, raps, and riddles that are popular with students and may hook some of them who aren't interested in traditional, rhymed verse by well-known poets. (Sometimes, teaching reading through a rap can be motivating to some reluctant, struggling readers. Don't miss this opportunity to turn them on to reading! However, be aware that some popular raps can be inappropriate for school.)

Some favorite read-aloud books that are now considered poetry:

- *A My Name Is Alice* by Jane Bayer (Dial, 1984) K–2
- *Alpha Beta Chowder* by Jeanne Steig (HarperCollins, 1992) K–5
- *Aster Aardvark's Alphabet Adventures* by Steven Kellogg (HarperTrophy, 1992) K–5
- *Busy Buzzing Bumblebees and Other Tongue Twisters* by Alvin Schwartz (HarperTrophy, 1992) K–5
- *A Chocolate Moose for Dinner* by Fred Gwynne (Aladdin, 1988) 2–5
- *Jamberry* by Bruce Degen (HarperTrophy, 1985) K–2
- *The King Who Rained* by Fred Gwynne (Aladdin, 1988) 2–5
- *One Sun: A Book of Terse Verse* by Bruce McMillan (Holiday House, 1992) 3–5
- *Palindromania!* by Jon Agee (Farrar, Straus and Giroux, 2002) 3–5
- *Westward Ho Ho Ho! Jokes from the Wild West* by Victoria Hartman (Puffin, 1994) 3–5
- *Yours Till Banana Splits: 201 Autograph Rhymes* by Joanna Cole and Stephanie Calmenson (HarperTrophy, 1995) 3–5
- *The Z Was Zapped: A Play in Twenty-Six Acts* by Chris Van Allsburg (Houghton Mifflin, 1987) 2–5

Picture Books with Rhyming Text

Some picture books are simply books of poetry. The story or message is written in rhymed verse that makes it fun to read aloud and discuss. These books may seem like simple reading to students in grades two through five, but they are just right as models of poetry students can imitate and write. Jamie Lee Curtis and her illustrator, Laura Cornell, have several books like this, as does Katie Couric.

- *Annie Bananie* by Leah Komaiko (HarperTrophy, 2003)

- *The Brand New Kid* by Katie Couric (Doubleday, 2000)

- *The Crayon Box That Talked* by Shane DeRolf (Random House Books for Young Readers, 1997)

- *How I Spent My Summer Vacation* by Mark Teague (Dragonfly Books, 1997)

- *I'm Gonna Like Me: Letting Off a Little Self-Esteem* by Jamie Lee Curtis (Joanna Cotler Books, 2002)

- *Little Miss Spider* by David Kirk (Scholastic Press, 2003)

- *Loud Lips Lucy* by Tolya L. Thompson (Savor Publishing, 2001)

- *My Daddy and I* by P. K. Hallinan (Ideals Children's Books, 2006)

- *My Little Sister Ate One Hare* by Bill Grossman (Dragonfly Books, 1998)

- *The Night Before Easter* by Natasha Wing (Grosset & Dunlap, 1999)

- *The Night Before Summer Vacation* by Natasha Wing (Grosset & Dunlap, 2002)

- *The Night Before the Tooth Fairy* by Natasha Wing (Grosset & Dunlap, 2003)

- *The Night Before Valentine's Day* by Natasha Wing (Grosset & Dunlap, 2001)

- *Over in the Meadow: A Counting Rhyme* by Olive A. Wadsworth (North-South Books, 2002)

- *Today I Feel Silly & Other Moods That Make My Day* by Jamie Lee Curtis (Joanna Cotler Books, 1998)

- *'Twas the Night Before Thanksgiving* by Dav Pilkey (Scholastic, 2004)

- *Where Do Balloons Go? An Uplifting Mystery* by Jamie Lee Curtis (Joanna Cotler Books, 2000)

Teaching Reading with Poetry

Guided Reading does not simply mean reading leveled readers and other leveled text as some educators believe. The International Reading Association has a broader definition for Guided Reading: reading instruction in which the teacher provides the structure and purpose for reading and for responding to the material read (Harris and Hodges, 1995).

In most schools, students read lots of fiction and nonfiction during Guided Reading. Teachers vary the genres because fiction and nonfiction have different formats and call for different reading skills and strategies. However, plays, poetry, and directions have their own unique structures. To understand these, students need to use comprehension skills and strategies that are different from those they use with stories and information. So, to meet the goals of teaching **all** of the comprehension skills and strategies necessary to read, enjoy, and learn from all of the different kinds of texts, students need to have instruction and practice in reading different kinds of text, including poetry. A variety of materials is also essential to meet the goal of developing students' background knowledge, meaning vocabularies, and oral language. In addition, children enjoy the change of pace that poetry provides, as well as the special activities you can do with poetry. Students not only enjoy but can learn from reading poetry aloud, reading poetry in echo or choral reading formats, and drawing pictures of what they visualize as they read poetry.

Reading and discussing a poem as a class is an important part of the elementary curriculum. It also can be an enjoyable part! Since there is no need for grouping with poetry lessons, the whole class can do the before-, during-, and after-reading activities together. Everyone can read and enjoy poetry, so no student needs to be kept "busy" while a few others participate in the lesson. Teachers can help emergent readers succeed at reading poetry by using a shared reading or an echo- and choral-reading format. These reading formats need not be confined to kindergarten and early first grade.

Shared Reading

Shared reading provides opportunities for teachers to model and interact with students, showing them how to think as they read. If a teacher writes a poem on a large piece of chart paper or overhead transparency, all of the students can see the print and any pictures the teacher has drawn. Then, the teacher can also focus the students' attention on whatever strategy is being taught or developed in the lesson. As they do with the shared reading of big books, teachers in grades two through five should find and use poetry students can read and enjoy. That way, teachers can demonstrate and "think-aloud" as they introduce new comprehension strategies. For students in grades two through five who are further along in their reading skills, shared reading of poetry provides opportunities to learn many new words, build concepts, and practice comprehension strategies. There is truly something for everyone in a good reading lesson with poetry, and, consequently, it can be considered a "multilevel" activity. **Multilevel** means that there are multiple things to be learned in the lesson, and the teacher interacts in different ways with individual children in the class during the reading and discussion of the poem.

Echo and Choral Reading

Echo and choral reading are two other excellent during-reading formats to use with students when doing Guided Reading lessons. **Echo reading** is when the teacher reads a line (or lines) and students become the echo, reading after the teacher or repeating what the teacher reads. After one or two readings of a poem, students can do a **choral reading**. Now, the teacher and students (or groups of students) read different lines or verses. Echo and choral reading allow all children to be active participants in the reading lesson. All students, at every grade level, can benefit from echo and choral reading, especially when reading poetry.

When preparing for choral reading, select a poem and copy it on chart paper or an overhead transparency or make an individual copy for each student. Then, decide how much you will read and how much students will read. Finally, rehearse the poem several times so that students will understand the tempo, which words are stressed, when they should raise and lower their voices, and when and how long to pause. With every reading of the poem, students will become more fluent readers and gain more confidence.

After reading a poem, students should have an opportunity to respond to what they have read. Sometimes, the response is brief with students discussing the poem informally, sharing connections to their own lives, or expressing whether they liked the poem. Sometimes, there may be time for students to illustrate the poem, memorize it, or write about it. Sometimes, children may write poetry of their own in the same style or form as the poem that was read.

Guided Reading Lessons

Here are some good read-aloud poems by Shel Silverstein (see pages 10–11) that work just as well for Guided Reading lessons:

- "Smart"
- "Sarah Cynthia Sylvia Stout Would Not Take the Garbage Out"
- "Benjamin Bunnn"
- "Homework Machine"
- "Whatif"
- "The Fly Is In"

After preparing the selected poem (write it for everyone to see or make copies), read the poem to students and talk about what happens in the poem—what the poem is about. The second reading can be an echo reading (page 15). Ask students to be ready to tell you their favorite parts after this reading. If students want to read the poem again (or if you have time and want them to), have students do a choral reading. Remember to decide who will read which lines. You can end the lesson with students illustrating the poem!

Here is an example of a Guided Reading lesson with the poem "Band-Aids" by Shel Silverstein.

First/Second Reading

Before Reading: Talk about Band-Aids®, when to use them, and why. Tell the class about a time or times you used Band-Aids® as a child and whether you use them now (text-to-self connections). Let students make connections and tell the class their Band-Aid® stories.

During Reading: Ask students to **listen** for all of the places the person in the poem uses Band-Aids®. Read the poem to the class. Next, have students read with you, joining in and sharing the reading of this humorous poem.

After Reading: Discuss where the person in the poem put Band-Aids®. Ask students, "Did he need them?"

Third Reading

Before Reading: Tell students, "This time, you will read "Band-Aids" with partners. As you read the poem with your partners, one person will read and the other person will count how many Band-Aids® are used in the poem." Explain that they can read the poem more than once if they need to. After reading the poem, they are to discuss the number of Band-Aids® they counted with their partners.

During Reading: For partner reading of the poem, have one partner read the poem while the other partner listens and counts Band-Aids®. As the partners read, circulate around the classroom, listening and helping if needed.

After Reading: Discuss how many Band-Aids® were used on the person in this poem. If there is time, have students draw the person with all of those Band-Aids®!

Writing Poetry

When reading poetry **to** students during a teacher read-aloud or reading poetry **with** students during a Guided Reading lesson, remind them that they can also **write** poetry. There are always some students who find poetry fascinating and can do a good job of mimicking the poetry they read. These same students often write some wonderful poetry of their own. Young children enjoy writing funny verses, using vivid word pictures, making powerful comparisons, and expressing deep sentiment. These are all important skills for good writing. For some children, writing poetry is more fun than reading it! Here are some easy writing lessons for poetry.

Rhymed Verse

Rhymed verse is the most familiar kind of poetry to most young students, but for many students, it is the hardest to write! Some students know how to write words that rhyme but often cannot put them into meaningful lines that make sense. When given the right topic—a familiar one—this sometimes becomes an easier task for students.

Crayon

by Katie Chinlund, Annie Young, and Emily Johnson

If I were a crayon,
I'd be the brightest of them all.
Kids could use me all day long
For projects big and small.
If I were a crayon,
I'd create all kinds of animals—
    a fish, a tiger, or a dog.
I'd draw all types of weather—
    sunshine, rain, or fog.
Crayons are fun to use;
They keep me smiling for hours,
As I draw what I want—
    cars, trains, or flowers.

School

by Turner Chambliss

I love school. School is fun.
I am sad when the week is done.
I laugh and learn, run and play.
School is where I want to stay.
I make new friends and learn new things.
Fun is what school always brings.
I do lots of work, but it's okay.
My teacher makes school fun—hooray!

See pages 35–36 and transparencies A–B for illustrated versions of "Crayon" and "School."

Acrostic Poems Using Names

For an easy lesson early in the year, let students use their names to write acrostic poems. Later in the year, students can use book characters, holidays, science or social studies themes, or names of places for subject matter. Here are some examples of acrostic poems using names to share with students:

Jennifer
by Jennifer Place

Joyful
Excellent
Nice
Nurturing
Intelligent
Fantastic
Enthusiastic
Radical

Amanda
by Amanda Gordon

Animal Lover
Marvelous
Admirable
Nice
Diligent
Always on the go

Rory
by Rory Gavin

Rare
Outstanding
Radical
Youthful

Amelia
by Amelia Rogers

Awesome
Magnificent
Elegant
Lovely
Inspiring
Amazing

See page 37 and transparency C for "Rory" and "Amelia."

Emily

by Emily Johnson

Enthusiastic
Magnificent
Intriguing
Loveable
Young

For a writing lesson that also helps with vocabulary building, let each student write an acrostic poem with his own name. Then, have him use the dictionary to see if he can find any "better" or more descriptive words. During this process, students often find and learn some meaningful words that begin with the letters in their names.

The student thinks of words for each letter in his name.

Stephen

Smart
Thin
Energetic
Polite
Handsome
Exact
Nice

Then, the student uses a dictionary to find better, more descriptive words.

Stephen

Sagacious
Trustworthy
Extraordinary
Punctual
Humanitarian
Exurbanite
Nocturnal

Acrostic Poems Using Themes or Holidays

Thanksgiving

Thankful
Happy
Autumn
Native Americans
Kind
Safe
Giving
Invited
Valued
Inspiring
New World
Grateful

Spring

Sunny
Plants
Rain
Insects
Nature
Growing

See page 38 and transparency D for an illustrated version of "Thanksgiving."

Cinquains

Writing cinquains is a favorite of teachers and students. A cinquain usually consists of five unrhymed lines that are made up of two, four, six, eight, and two syllables. Some classes may need to start with a simplified variation, using five unrhymed lines that are made up of one word, two words, three words, four words, and one word.

First, read a cinquain **to** students. Next, explain the form used for writing cinquains to students and call their attention to each part of the poem as you reread it. Then, discuss what students will write and why. Finally, have each student think, follow the directions, and write a cinquain. Here is a cinquain using the simple variation:

Author's Note: I wrote this cinquain about New York City, my favorite place to visit with my daughter, Suzanne.

City

City
New York
Busy, crowded, noisy
Shopping, watching, eating, hurrying
Fun!

See page 39 and transparency E for an illustrated version of "City."

Here are some cinquains written by students in a language arts methods class at Wake Forest University on a day they were talking about teaching poetry. These students used the traditional pattern for their cinquains.

Seashore

by Katie Chinlund

Seashore
sunny, sandy
swimming, shopping, surfing
constant state of relaxation
flip-flops

See page 39 and transparency E for an illustrated version of "Seashore."

Tennis

by Annie Young

Tennis
sweating, racquet
running, jumping, falling
constant motion to win the match
tennis

Weekend

by Amanda Gordon, Melanie Schneider, and Rory Gavin

Weekend
fun, relaxing
cheering, sleeping, playing
time off from school to rest at last
a break

Ice Cream

by Emily Johnson

Ice cream
Cold and creamy
Quickly dripping, melting
The flavor of it lasting on
My tongue

See page 40 and transparency F for an illustrated version of "Ice Cream."

Haiku

Haiku is an ancient form of Japanese poetry. Each haiku consists of seventeen syllables arranged in a five-seven-five pattern. Haiku generally refer to nature, something happening at the moment, or an emotion or feeling. Although haiku is a favorite of teachers, it is not always a favorite of students. Have fun writing haiku with your class but be aware that not all students may enjoy this activity as much as you do!

Fall

by Kandace Wernsing, Katie Beaver, Katherine Cardwell, and Martha Ripple

Leaves; red, brown, yellow
Dying leaves fall to the ground
Then, I must rake them.

Mountains

by Amelia Rogers, Lorah Hoft, Turner Chambliss, and Katie Ball

The humps, the big humps
Lovely little humps of rock
I love the mountains!

See page 41 and transparency G for illustrated versions of "Fall" and "Mountains."

Definition or List Poems

Other good types of poems for student writing are definition or list poems. In a definition poem, the lines define the topic of the poem. In a list poem, the poem is basically a list of words associated with the topic of the poem. Here are some wonderful examples:

Gold
by Amelia Rogers, Katie Ball, Jennifer Place, Turner Chambliss, and Lorah Hoft

Gold is the necklace
    blinging 'round my neck.
Gold are the earrings
    dangling from my ears.
Gold are the wedding bands
    around my parents' fingers.
Gold is the tooth
    in my brother's mouth.

See page 42 and transparency H for an illustrated version of "Gold."

Girl–Boy
by Anna Shaw, Pattie Gabbert, and Annie Ward

Girl
compassionate, talkative
laughing, dancing, playing
jewelry, dresses, sports, sweat
grunting, wrestling, eating
funny, helpful
Boy

See page 43 and transparency I for an illustrated version of "Girl–Boy."

© Carson-Dellosa

Life

by Lenora Simpson, Payton Deal, Rebecca Hix, and Stephen Lyday

Life is dancing in the rain.

Life is trudging.

Life is a storm.

Life is a rainbow after the storm.

Life is learning.

Life is laughing.

Life is standing on top of a mountain,
   looking for miles and miles.

Life is a puzzle.

Life is breathing.

Life is musical.

Life is living.

See page 44 and transparency J for an illustrated version of "Life."

I Wish

by Katherine Cardwell, Katie Beaver, Kandace Wernsing, and Martha Ripple

I wish I were an author

Who wrote beautiful books,

Who made children love to read,

And teachers love to teach.

Maybe today I will get my wish,

And wake up a famous author,

And then I will be as happy as can be!

See page 45 and transparency K for an illustrated version of "I Wish."

Happy

by Rory Gavin, Melanie Schneider, and Amanda Gordon

Sounds like birds chirping
Looks like perfect pearly whites
Tastes like heaven
Feels like floating
Smells like a rose garden
I'm almost giddy!

Concrete Poems

When writing concrete poems, young poets create pictures by arranging words. These word picture poems can be a single word, a string of words, or a sentence arranged to make a picture. Here are some examples to share with your students:

Pizza

by Pattie Gabbert

pizza pizza pizza pizza pizza pizza
cheese cheese cheese cheese cheese
cheese cheese cheese cheese cheese
cheese cheese cheese cheese
cheese pepperoni cheese sausage
cheese cheese cheese cheese
onion cheese pepper cheese
cheese cheese cheese
pepperoni cheese cheese
cheese sausage
cheese pepperoni
onion cheese ch
cheese cheese
cheese cheese
cheese onion
cheese
cheese
cheese

Star

by Kandace Wernsing

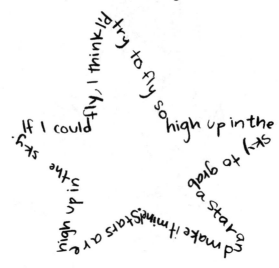

See page 46 and transparency L for an illustrated version of "Star."

Bear in the Grass

by Jennifer Place

Corduroy

by Katherine Cardwell

© Carson-Dellosa

A Reading/Writing Lesson Using Rhymed Verse

(Katherine Cardwell taught this lesson to a third-grade class at Vienna Elementary School in Pfafftown, North Carolina.)

Before Reading: To begin the lesson, the teacher passes out one of her favorite poems to students. The title of the poem is "Mr. Nobody," written by an anonymous poet. She tells students, "I loved this poem when I was young, and my dad read it to me."

Mr. Nobody
Anonymous

I know a funny little man,
As quiet as a mouse,
Who does the mischief that is done
In everybody's house!
There's no one ever sees his face,
And yet we all agree
That every plate we break was cracked
By Mr. Nobody

'Tis he who always tears our books,
Who leaves the door ajar,
He pulls the buttons from our shirts,
And scatters pins afar;
That squeaking door will always squeak
For, prithee, don't you see,
We leave the oiling to be done
By Mr. Nobody.

He puts damp wood upon the fire,
That kettle cannot boil;
His are the feet that bring in mud,
And all the carpets soil.
The papers always are mislaid,
Who had them last but he?
There's no one tosses them about
But Mr. Nobody.

The finger marks upon the door
By none of us are made;
We never leave the blinds unclosed,
To let the curtains fade;
The ink we never spill; the boots
That lying round you see
Are not our boots; they all belong
To Mr. Nobody.

First, the teacher tells students to listen as she reads the poem to them. After she
has read it aloud to them, they discuss the poem line by line. Next, the teacher asks,
"When do you think this poem was written—now or long ago? What are some clues in
the poem?" (Students say "the kettle boiling on the fire" and "inkwells" to support the
conclusion that it was written long ago.) The teacher talks about the verses, or stanzas,
and the lines in the poem. Then, she has students find and count the number of lines
in different verses.

During Reading: Next, the teacher asks students to chorally read the poem **with** her.
Children read quietly, and the teacher takes the lead with a strong voice. Then, they
read the poem again. This time, students are more comfortable and read it with equally
strong voices—a true shared reading.

After Reading: A question follows the choral readings of this poem: "Does this poem rhyme?" Children respond that some of the lines rhyme but not all of them. The teacher asks about specific lines from the poem. Students give a thumbs-up if the lines rhyme and a thumbs-down if the lines don't rhyme. Then, students find the rhyming words. Finally, the teacher calls their attention to lines 2 and 4 and lines 6 and 8 in each verse. The lesson ends with a writing assignment. The teacher tells students, "Write another stanza for this poem. Be sure that lines 2 and 4 rhyme and lines 6 and 8 rhyme."

Crayon

by Annie Young, Emily Johnson, and Katie Chinlund

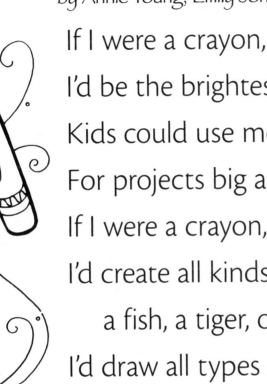

If I were a crayon,

I'd be the brightest of them all.

Kids could use me all day long

For projects big and small.

If I were a crayon,

I'd create all kinds of animals—

    a fish, a tiger, or a dog.

I'd draw all types of weather—

    sunshine, rain, or fog.

Crayons are fun to use;

They keep me smiling for hours,

As I draw what I want—

    cars, trains, or flowers.

School

by Turner Chambliss

I love school. School is fun.

I am sad when the week is done.

I laugh and learn, run and play.

School is where I want to stay.

I make new friends and learn new things.

Fun is what school always brings.

I do lots of work, but it's okay.

My teacher makes school fun—hooray!

Rory

by Rory Gavin

Rare

Outstanding

Radical

Youthful

Amelia

by Amelia Rogers

Awesome

Magnificent

Elegant

Lovely

Inspiring

Amazing

Thankful

Happy

Autumn

Native Americans

Kind

Safe

Giving

Invited

Valued

Inspiring

New World

Grateful

City

New York

Busy, crowded, noisy

Shopping, watching, eating, hurrying

Fun!

Seashore

by Katie Chinlund

Seashore

sunny, sandy

swimming, shopping, surfing

constant state of relaxation

flip-flops

by Emily Johnson

Ice cream
Cold and creamy
Quickly dripping, melting
The flavor of it lasting on
My tongue

Fall

by Kandace Wernsing, Katie Beaver, Katherine Cardwell, and Martha Ripple

Leaves; red, brown, yellow
Dying leaves fall to the ground
Then, I must rake them.

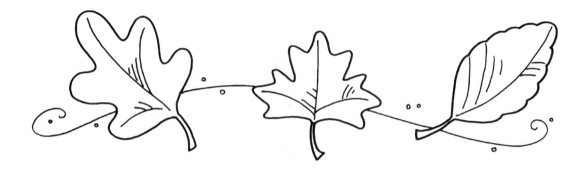

Mountains

by Amelia Rogers, Lorah Hoft, Turner Chambliss, and Katie Ball

The humps, the big humps
Lovely little humps of rock
I love the mountains!

Gold

by Amelia Rogers, Katie Ball, Jennifer Place, Turner Chambliss, and Lorah Hoft

Gold is the necklace
  blinging 'round my neck.
Gold are the earrings
  dangling from my ears.
Gold are the wedding bands
  around my parents' fingers.
Gold is the tooth
  in my brother's mouth.

  Poetry for Reading and Writing • CD-104233

by Anna Shaw, Pattie Gabbert, and Annie Ward

Girl
compassionate, talkative
laughing, dancing, playing
jewelry, dresses, sports, sweat
grunting, wrestling, eating
funny, helpful
Boy

by Lenora Simpson, Payton Deal, Rebecca Hix, and Stephen Lyday

Life is dancing in the rain.

Life is trudging.

Life is a storm.

Life is a rainbow after the storm.

Life is learning.

Life is laughing.

Life is standing on top of a mountain,
    looking for miles and miles.

Life is a puzzle.

Life is breathing.

Life is musical.

Life is living.

by Katherine Cardwell, Katie Beaver, Kandace Wernsing, and Martha Ripple

I wish I were an author,

Who wrote beautiful books,

Who made children love to read,

And teachers love to teach.

Maybe today I will get my wish,

And wake up a famous author,

And then I will be as happy as can be!

Star

by Kandace Wernsing

If I could fly, I think I'd try to fly so high up in the sky to grab a star and make it mine. Stars are high up in the sky.

References

Children's Books

The 20th Century Children's Poetry Treasury selected by Jack Prelutsky (Knopf Books for Young Readers, 1999)

A My Name Is Alice by Jane Bayer (Dial, 1984)

Alpha Beta Chowder by Jeanne Steig (HarperCollins, 1992)

Aster Aardvark's Alphabet Adventures by Steven Kellogg (HarperTrophy, 1992)

Annie Bananie by Leah Komaiko (HarperTrophy, 2003)

The Brand New Kid by Katie Couric (Doubleday, 2000)

Busy Buzzing Bumblebees and Other Tongue Twisters by Alvin Schwartz (HarperTrophy, 1992)

Cat Poems selected by Myra Cohn Livingston (Holiday House, 1987)

A Child's Garden of Verses by Robert Louis Stevenson (Simon & Schuster Children's Publishing, 1999)

A Chocolate Moose for Dinner by Fred Gwynne (Aladdin, 1988)

The Crayon Box That Talked by Shane DeRolf (Random House Books for Young Readers, 1997)

How I Spent My Summer Vacation by Mark Teague (Dragonfly Books, 1997)

I'm Gonna Like Me: Letting Off a Little Self-Esteem by Jamie Lee Curtis (Joanna Cotler Books, 2002)

Jamberry by Bruce Degen (HarperTrophy, 1985)

The King Who Rained by Fred Gwynne (Aladdin, 1988)

A Light in the Attic by Shel Silverstein (HarperCollins, 1981)

Little Miss Spider by David Kirk (Scholastic Press, 2003)

Loud Lips Lucy by Tolya L. Thompson (Savor Publishing, 2001)

My Daddy and I by P. K. Hallinan (Ideals Children's Books, 2006)

My Little Sister Ate One Hare by Bill Grossman (Dragonfly Books, 1998)

The Night Before Easter by Natasha Wing (Grosset & Dunlap, 1999)

The Night Before Summer Vacation by Natasha Wing (Grosset & Dunlap, 2002)

The Night Before the Tooth Fairy by Natasha Wing (Grosset & Dunlap, 2003)

The Night Before Valentine's Day by Natasha Wing (Grosset & Dunlap, 2001)

One Sun: A Book of Terse Verse by Bruce McMillan (Holiday House, 1992)

Over in the Meadow: A Counting Rhyme by Olive A. Wadsworth (North-South Books, 2002)

Palindromania! by Jon Agee (Farrar, Straus and Giroux, 2002)

Poetry for Young People: Carl Sandburg edited by Frances Schoonmaker Bolin (Sterling, 1995)

Poetry for Young People: Edgar Allan Poe edited by Brod Bagert (Sterling, 1995)

Poetry for Young People: Emily Dickinson edited by Frances Schoonmaker Bolin (Sterling, 1994)

Poetry for Young People: Robert Frost edited by Gary D. Schmidt (Sterling, 1994)

Poetry for Young People: Walt Whitman edited by Jonathan Levin (Sterling, 1997)

Poetry for Young People: William Carlos Williams edited by Christopher MacGowan (Sterling, 2003)

The Random House Book of Poetry for Children selected by Jack Prelutsky (Random House Books for Young Readers, 2000)

Today I Feel Silly & Other Moods That Make My Day by Jamie Lee Curtis (Joanna Cotler Books, 1998)

'Twas the Night Before Thanksgiving by Dav Pilkey (Scholastic, 2004)

Westward Ho Ho Ho! Jokes from the Wild West by Victoria Hartman (Puffin, 1994)

Where Do Balloons Go? An Uplifting Mystery by Jamie Lee Curtis (Joanna Cotler Books, 2000)

Where the Sidewalk Ends by Shel Silverstein (HarperCollins, 1974)

Yours Till Banana Splits: 201 Autograph Rhymes by Joanna Cole and Stephanie Calmenson (HarperTrophy, 1995)

The Z Was Zapped: A Play in Twenty-Six Acts by Chris Van Allsburg (Houghton Mifflin, 1987)

Zoo Doings: Animal Poems by Jack Prelutsky (Greenwillow Books, 1983)

Professional Resources

Harris, T. L., and R. E. Hodges, eds. 1995. *The Literacy Dictionary.* Newark, DE: International Reading Association.